D0021385

CATCH!
BATTLE!
COLLECT!

MINI HACKS FOR

PokéMon
GO players

CATCHING

CATCH!
BATTLE!
COLLECT!

MINI HACKS FOR

PokéMon

GO players

CATCHING

SKILLS, TIPS, AND TECHNIQUES FOR CAPTURING MONSTERS

JUSTIN RYAN

Sky Pony Press
New York

Copyright © 2016 by Hollan Publishing, Inc.

All rights reserved. No part of this book may be reproduced in any manner without the express written consent of the publisher, except in the case of brief excerpts in critical reviews or articles. All inquiries should be addressed to Sky Pony Press, 307 West 36th Street, 11th Floor, New York, NY 10018.

Sky Pony Press books may be purchased in bulk at special discounts for sales promotion, corporate gifts, fund-raising, or educational purposes. Special editions can also be created to specifications. For details, contact the Special Sales Department, Sky Pony Press, 307 West 36th Street, 11th Floor, New York, NY 10018 or info@skyhorsepublishing.com.

Sky Pony® is a registered trademark of Skyhorse Publishing, Inc.®, a Delaware corporation.

Visit our website at www.skyponypress.com.

10 9 8 7 6 5 4 3 2 1

Library of Congress Cataloging-in-Publication Data is available on file.

Cover design by Brian Peterson
Book design by Joshua Barnaby

Print ISBN: 978-1-5107-2210-1
Ebook ISBN: 978-1-5107-2212-5

Printed in The United States of America

TABLE OF CONTENTS

MINI HACKS FOR

PokéMon

GO players

CATCHING

INTRODUCTION

Charmander letting
out a mighty growl.

Pokémon GO is a place where you can battle different monsters, visit new and exciting maps, and collect hundreds of items. But beyond all the adventures you will find yourself embarking on, one of the most fulfilling will be catching Pokémon, encountering different types of monsters, and using your best catching skills to add them to your collection.

A Paras just waiting to be captured.

Ekans chilling on the sidewalk.

It's why "Catch 'em all" is so commonly heard in Pokémon games—because catching all of these wild and diverse monsters is so challenging, but also, so much fun. And in Pokémon GO, you have the opportunity to capture these monsters immediately on your phone, right then and there.

Getting ready to throw my Poké Ball at this Rattata.

Successfully made contact and now Ekans is being transported into my Poké Ball.

I overthrew my shot at this Squirtle.

You could be on the Ferris wheel at an amusement park catching a Pokémon, or you could be at a concert or a movie when a monster makes an appearance. That's why you should always be ready to catch, and have the necessary skills to be a master catcher when you play the game.

Geodude getting a bite to eat at the food court.

Meowth looking for a mouse to catch on the bus.

Cubone refusing to get out of the street.

This book will go over things like how to use the map, how and when to use incenses and lures, where to find certain types of Pokémon, how to hatch eggs to get more Pokémon, and the act of catching itself, so you'll be ready and prepared whenever that rare Pokémon you've been wanting peeks its head around the corner.

We'll go over how PokéStops like these can help you gain items.

How different Poké Balls and items can help make catching easier.

Sometimes you won't catch the monster you want, even after doing everything right. And other times you still might mess up your throw, or not do something correctly. But you should be able to succeed at catching with the help of these different tips and hacks. And if you follow this book correctly, there's no reason why you can't catch 'em all.

What are you waiting for? There are Pokémon to catch! Let's go!

How catching can help you gain XP and level up.

And how to perfect your throw so you don't lose out on Pokémon you really want.

CHAPTER 1
CATCHING YOUR FIRST POKÉMON

After you select your trainer in the game and customize their appearance, you'll have the opportunity to catch a Charmander, Squirtle or Bulbasaur.

Here you can see the starter Pokémon on the map.

These starter Pokémon are a good introduction into the world of types, where each Pokémon has its own unique type associated with it (some even have more than one). Bulbasaur is a grass-and-poison-type Pokémon, Charmander is a fire-type Pokémon, and Squirtle is a water-type. These specific types will play a lot more into the game when you actually battle Pokémon. But for right now, think of types as categories when you're catching monsters.

Here is more detailed info about each of the starter Pokémon.

Right now though, you'll only have the ability to catch one of them. There will be other opportunities to catch them later in the game, but for right now, choose one which you like the most and think is best.

Bulbasaur isn't going down without a fight.

After you select which Pokémon you want to catch, you will be taken to a screen where the Pokémon will be standing in the middle, and a Poké Ball will be floating down at the bottom of your phone.

Charmander is trying to dodge my throws.

Looks like Squirtle's trying to intimidate me a bit.

All you have to do to catch them is throw the ball at the Pokémon, make contact with it, watch your Pokémon disappear into the ball, and then watch as the ball moves back and forth. If a "Gotcha!" message appears, this means that you've successfully captured your monster. Now that Pokémon will appear in your menu.

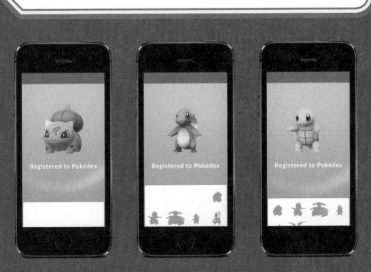

The starter Pokémon after being caught.

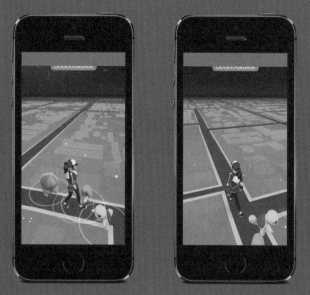

Here all of the starters are in plain sight.

If Charmander, Squirtle, or Bulbasaur don't appeal to you, you can also catch a Pikachu as your first Pokémon, but it will take a little more work. When you see the three Pokémon appear on the screen, walk away from them so you can't see them anymore.

But now I've started to walk away and they aren't in view.

Oh hello there, Pikachu!

They should then reappear in front of you. Do this a few more times and Pikachu should reappear with them when they come back.

Pikachu wasn't hard to catch at all, and is now in my collection.

Now that you have your first Pokémon, we can locate it in two different places: the Pokémon menu and the Pokédex. The Pokémon menu shows you all the monsters you've captured, their statistics, their attacks, and even gives you the ability to rename them.

Here is the Pokémon menu, where you can
see a lot of the monsters I've captured.

You can reorganize this list by recently-captured Pokémon, favorites, names, or other ways. Slide, or touch, the egg menu at the right, where you can see all the eggs you have, if you are incubating any, and how long you have to travel until they hatch.

Here is what my egg menu looks like. You can see I'm incubating three eggs right now.

The Pokédex is a bit different from the Pokémon menu. The Pokédex shows you the numbers for all the potential monsters you can collect in the game, which Pokémon you already have caught, evolved or hatched, and which you've encountered in the wild but failed to catch. In this case, a silhouette of the Pokémon is shown. If you click on a Pokémon, you'll see more detailed information, like how many you've seen, how many you've caught, and a description of what that Pokémon is like.

The Pokédex shows me not just what Pokémon I have, but also how many I still need to catch.

The Pokémon menu shows you all of the Pokémon you have, while the Pokédex shows you a more detailed breakdown of each Pokémon. You could have twenty Bulbasaurs or fifty Dragonites, but you'll only see these monsters appear once in the Pokédex. The Pokédex is a good way to keep track of how many more Pokémon you want and still need to catch, while the Pokémon menu gives you more specific information about the Pokémon you already have.

CHAPTER 2
MASTERING YOUR THROW

Catching is the fundamental action of Pokémon GO; all other things aren't quite as important. You can get new Pokémon by hatching eggs or evolving the ones you already have, but catching is still going to be your primary way of collecting new monsters. Visiting PokéStops is a great way to learn about new parts of your city, but their best purpose is getting you items for catching, or for setting out a lure to catch more Pokémon. If you want to go to a gym to battle, you'll need Pokémon, and you get those from catching. It's at the very heart of the game, and is one of the most exciting and challenging aspects of Pokémon GO.

Every encounter with a Pokémon is a chance to try something new.

But when you're in a catching scenario, it's more than just flicking a ball at the Pokémon. There are a lot of different factors at play that will determine whether or not you capture a monster, and how much XP you will get from it. This chapter will show you how to become very good at this important skill.

THROWING THE BALL

When you're face-to-face with your Pokémon, you'll see the Poké Ball bouncing up and down in front of you. To throw it, touch the Poké Ball with your thumb or finger, and swipe it up at the Pokémon. The ball will GO as far as you throw it, and it will probably take a few times to get your throw just right.

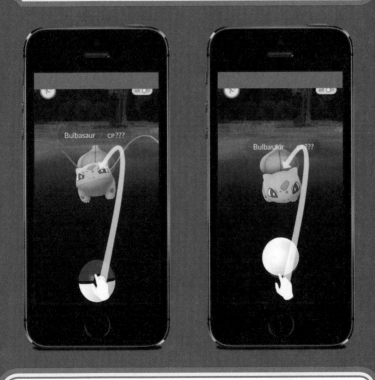

Capturing your first starter Pokémon will give you a pretty good idea of what goes into catching.

You'll have to remember how far the ball went when you threw it, and if it went too far or not far at all, you'll have to readjust that for future throws. Sometimes, the Pokémon might be closer to the screen, and sometimes it might be closer to the back or top. You'll have to adjust your throw for this to make sure you make successful contact.

Growlithe is further away here, so I'll have to throw a bit farther.

But this starter Charmander is up close, so I'll have to throw a bit softer.

There are a lot of different methods for you to throw your ball that can help you catch Pokémon and find your right style. Just like pitchers in baseball know a lot of different ways to throw a ball to the catcher, there are a lot of ways you can incorporate different throws into the game. Throwing in a straight line from bottom to top is an easy way to keep track of your throw and keep it centered.

This shot is lined straight up with Sandshrew.

Same with this Rhydon.

You can also move the ball at the bottom of the screen to the left or right and then throw from a different angle at the Pokémon. You also don't have to throw directly at the Pokémon in a straight line. You can arc your shot so it travels in the air a bit more and then hits the Pokémon. Simply grab the ball, move it to the left or right as much as you please, and then create a curved path with your thumb or finger so it hits the Pokémon.

We're going to try throwing the ball from the left side of the screen for Rhydon here.

Also, try using different parts of your hand, or even throwing from a different part of the screen. If you throw mainly with your thumb, try with one or more of your fingers. If you throw with your thumb horizontally, try resting it so you're throwing from bottom to top. See what results you can get when you throw really fast vs. throwing slower. But make sure to experiment with all these different throwing methods, angles, and distances to see which works best. There isn't a best way of throwing in Pokémon GO—only the best way for you.

I'm going to try something different on Sandshrew as well.

It's also worth it to try throwing curveballs when you're catching Pokémon. These happen when you spin the ball in circles at the bottom of your screen and then throw. You can tell a curveball is coming if sparks start to shoot out of it.

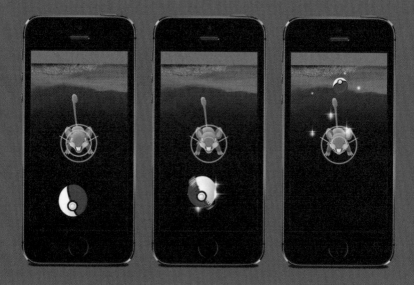

This Rattata got the curveball treatment.

Curveballs are harder to hit than regular throws because of their angles, and it's harder to tell where one will end up than if you had thrown straight. But just like any other throw, a curveball takes practice to master. Try taking a curveball to the bottom right corner of your screen and start spinning it to get it going. Then, take the ball and throw it in a "C" direction from the bottom, so you're coming up and around the Pokémon like the letter C. You can also try this in reverse from the left side of the screen.

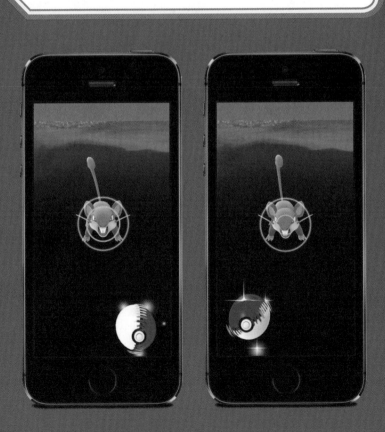

But if you nail it perfectly, the ball should travel in a curve with sparks shooting around it and hit your Pokémon. If you get this just right, you'll get an XP bonus. There isn't necessarily a huge advantage in catching a Pokémon with a curveball than with a regular throw—just bragging rights to show off that you know how to do it.

INFORMATION AND CIRCLES THAT APPEAR AROUND A POKÉMON.

When you grab your ball and get ready throw, you'll notice a few items. One of them are the letters CP with a number next to it. This represents that Pokémon's Combat Power, or CP level, and is a good indicator of how strong that Pokémon is. CP level is used more for battling, but it still works as a good way to tell if that will be a difficult Pokémon to catch in the wild. If it's a low CP, something between ten and a hundred, that means that the Pokémon will be easier to catch. If it's a higher CP, like above three hundred, that means that it'll be a bit more difficult, and may even require more throws than one, even if your first throw seemed perfect.

This Mankey is at a higher CP
so it might be more difficult to catch.

But this Venonat is at a much
lower one, making it easier.

I've thrown not-so-great throws at Pokémon with low CP and caught them on the very first try. But other times, I've thrown a perfect shot, right dead-center at a Pokémon with a higher CP, and didn't end up catching it.

This Rhydon should have been easier to catch, but it still managed to get away.

The important thing to notice when you grab the Poké Ball is a white circle that appears around the monster. You'll want your Poké Ball to hit the monster right in that circle for you to successfully capture it. You might be able to still make contact with the Pokémon, but the ball could bounce right off of it. That circle, though, should be the primary thing you aim at.

I went way too far left of the white circle when trying to catch this Mankey.

There will be times when you get it dead-center in the middle of the circle, and your Pokémon will still run away, and there will be other times when you throw a Poké Ball, and it just hits the edge of the circle but still manages to transport the monster inside. Aim for the circle to improve your chances.

Remember, just because a Pokémon was transported into your ball doesn't mean you caught it.

You'll need to wait for this message to confirm.

That white circle isn't the only thing you have to take into account when throwing. There's also another colored circle that serves as an indicator of how difficult this Pokémon will be to catch. This is called the target ring. The target ring can be colored green, orange, or red. Green means that the Pokémon is easier to catch, orange means that it is intermediate, and red means that it is very difficult.

Venonat's green ring means it's easier to catch.

Pidgey's yellow ring means it's intermediate.

This ring also starts off big, shrinks smaller until disappearing, and becomes big again. When the ring is at its smallest is the time when it's easiest to catch your Pokémon. When it's at its biggest is when it's going to be more difficult.

Pidgey's small target ring means that it'd be easier to catch right now.

But Venonat's big target ring means it'd be more difficult.

Remember, though, that although the ring moves when you're holding your ball, once you release it, it will stay that size until you make contact or your next shot happens.

I hit this Nidoran just right to get a Nice! shot.

There are also different bonuses you can get if you hit the target ring with your shot. If you hit the target ring when it's at its smallest, you can get an Excellent! shot. If you get it when it's about halfway sized, you can get a Great shot! If you get it when its much closer to the white circle, you can get a Nice! shot. These shots are more for bragging rights, so you don't have to worry about getting great shots for anything extra in the game, more as a way of letting you know that you had a really nice shot.

This is a lot to go over so far, so let's look again at the items and what they mean.

CP: How powerful that Pokémon is. Can also give idea of how hard it'll be to catch.

This high CP Growlithe was more difficult to catch.

But this low CP Pidgey was easier to come by.

White ring: The area on the monster you need your Poké Ball to hit.

I'll want to hit Growlithe right in
the center of that circle.

Target ring: The ring that tells you how difficult a Pokémon will be to catch. Green means easiest, while red is more difficult. Small ring means easier to catch while bigger means it's more difficult.

This Pidgey would be easier to catch than this Eevee, since the Pidgey has a green target ring.

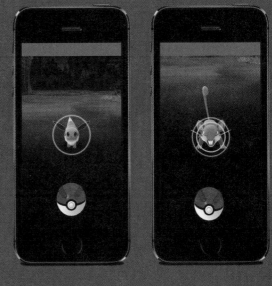

But this Eevee would be easier to catch than this Rattata, since Eevee's target ring is smaller.

While all of these aspects work in conjunction with each other, they don't necessarily determine on their own if a Pokémon will be easy or difficult to catch. You might encounter a more uncommon Pokémon, like Kabutops, who has a three-hundred-fifty CP and a red target ring, indicating that it's difficult to catch. However, you could throw an Excellent! shot when the target ring is small and catch the monster on your very first throw. There might be other times when you see another Pidgey roaming about with a green ring and medium level CP, but still can't manage to catch it even after a few solid throws. All of these items serve as good indicators for how difficult a Pokémon will be to catch, but at the end of the day, it's going to be how good your throw is that allows you to catch more monsters.

One important thing to remember: Augmented reality is fun, but can make catching difficult sometimes. You have to keep your phone still, and it's difficult to keep things focused. Don't be afraid to turn it off for more intense catching situations.

I wanted to take goofy pictures of these Pokémon, but I got distracted and wasn't able to catch them.

ITEMS AND DIFFERENT BALLS

When you're first starting out in the game, regular Poké Balls are the only balls you have to catch Pokémon, and they work pretty fine. But as you become more advanced in the game, a lot of the Pokémon you encounter will be harder to catch. You'll throw lots of balls at them and they'll run away pretty easily. But once you hit Level Twelve in the game, you'll be able to start using Great balls, items that make it easier to capture Pokémon when you encounter them in the wild. And when you reach Level Twenty, you'll gain access to Ultra balls, which are even more powerful than Great balls, and make it easier to catch Pokémon. These balls are more difficult to find in the wild than regular Poké Balls, and can't be bought in the shop, either. You actually have to find them if you want to use them.

I used Great balls here to catch Pokémon, even though a regular Poké Ball would have done the trick.

This brings up the question of when you should use a particular ball vs. another. Every catching situation is different, but there are some moments where you need to know for certain if it's better to use another ball or not.

1. IF IT'S A POKÉMON YOU REALLY WANT

Sure, you're going to want to save all the Great and Ultra balls that you possibly can and not be wasteful with them, but if there's a Pokémon that appears that you've been wanting for some time now, just use a Great or Ultra ball if you have one. Make sure you do your shot just right, though, and don't waste it.

2. IF THE POKÉMON HAS A RED TARGET RING AND A HIGH CP

These are indicators that the Pokémon will be difficult to catch, and depending on your level, will also influence how difficult the monster is to catch. If it's red, use a better ball, but if it's not, use a green one.

3. IF YOU ACTUALLY HAVE A LOT OF GREAT AND MASTER BALLS IN YOUR STOCK

Keeping a healthy supply of Poké Balls is a good idea, but at the end of the day, you'll want to actually use these Poké Balls to catch Pokémon, not let them just sit there. Save a few for those Pokémon you'll really want, and use regular Poké Balls when necessary, but don't be afraid to throw some Great or Ultra balls in regular catching scenarios.

RAZZ BERRIES

Razz Berries are an item that can be fed to a Pokémon before a throw that will make it easier to catch. You simply select the berry from the menu, give it to the Pokémon and voila, its effects are now working. You can use Razz Berries multiple times while trying to catch a Pokémon, but a single Razz Berry will only work for one throw. Razz Berries can start being collected once you reach Level Eight, and from there should become a regularly used item in your stock to catch Pokémon.

Here a Razz Berry helped me catch this Vulpix.

When all of these items and skills are used in conjunction, you'll be at your best catching ability. Advanced throwing skills, a healthy supply of regular, Great and Ultra balls, Razz Berries and knowing how to interpret target rings will make you a top-notch catcher. If there's one thing that's more important than all of these things, though, it's learning to perfect your throw. You can always get more Great and Ultra Balls, and you can encounter plenty of Pokémon in the game, but you'll really need to learn how to catch Pokémon and the best throw for you if you want to catch a lot of them.

Before you know it, you'll be catching Pokémon with top-notch shots in no time.

CHAPTER 3
USING THE MAP, LURES, INCENSE, AND POKÉSTOPS

Now that you're a throwing master, it's time to find Pokémon on the map to catch! This is the area where you'll be able to find all of the Pokémon you want to catch. During the day, the map is lit up a bright, light green with darker lines representing streets. At night, the map is a darker blue.

Here's the map during the day.

And here it is at night.

You'll also see little squares within those streets, which represent buildings. The map is based on wherever you are at that given moment, so a map in New York City will have a different layout than a map in Anchorage, Alaska.

This quiet neighborhood doesn't really have much going on in Pokémon GO.

But when I go downtown, things start to get more lively.

There is also a compass in the top right corner of the map, giving you a sense of direction where you are. You can also zoom in and zoom out to get a better perspective of where certain things might be.

An up-close zoom on the map.

And a view from further away. This bigger view allows me to see all of the things happening in my area.

Here is where you can also find PokéStops and see which ones have been powered up by lures. PokéStops are where you find you items that make catching easier, and will sometimes give you cool information about a landmark or neat area in your city.

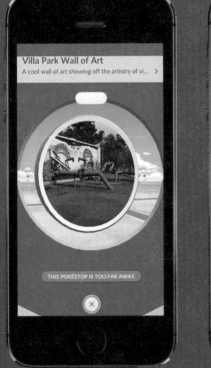

I walk by this art installation every week
but never knew what it was until I looked at this Pokestop.

To explore the map, all you need to do is start walking around, and you'll see your trainer start to move along, too. You can ride in a car with a trusted adult driving, which allows you to see the map moving by a lot faster than if you were walking. But you'll have less opportunity to catch a specific Pokémon since you'll be moving so fast.

It would have been cool to catch this Golbat or get Poké Balls from this Pokéstop, but I was moving too fast and couldn't stop at them.

In the map, there's also a Sightings menu that can serve as a good guide to catching Pokémon. Here you can see Pokémon that are in your area that you haven't caught, or have caught and can catch others like it. The Sightings menu is by no means perfect, though, and you can spend several minutes or hours trying to find a Pokémon you really want and still never see them.

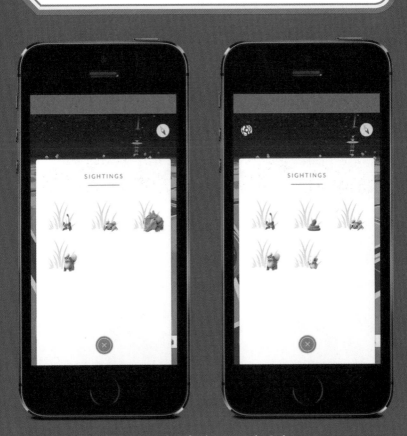

Although there are a lot of Pokémon in the Sightings menu, it's going to be difficult for me to find and catch all of them.

The Sightings menu is always changing, too, so one second it might display a Pidgeotto, and the next second it might display a Meowth. And there will be times when you're focusing on catching a specific Pokémon and encounter another Pokémon you still need to catch but weren't even thinking about. The Sightings menu is a good place to start for catching Pokémon, but still isn't a hundred-percent foolproof guide as to what monsters you might see in that area.

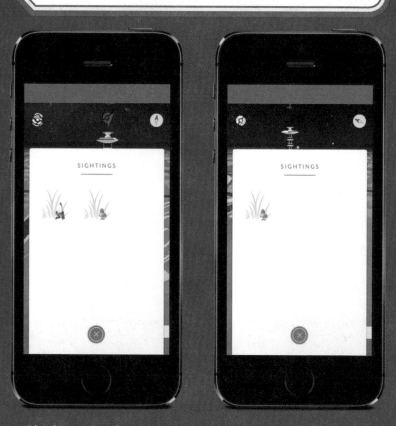

I barely moved ten feet and the menu for whatever is near me has changed.

An important thing to remember about the map is that where you are in real life will help determine what Pokémon show up. So if you're near the beach or a body of water, you might see a lot more water Pokémon than you would if you were in the mountains, where you might see a lot of ground or rock-type Pokémon. That's why moving around and exploring the map and different parts of your city or town is important to finding new Pokémon. Otherwise, you'll notice that you just see the same monsters over and over again where you are.

I play Pokémon GO in this area often and see a lot of Pidgeys and Rattatas. So it makes sense they're listed as nearby on this map,

There isn't necessarily a "best" area to find Pokémon, or a certain place in the world where, if you traveled, you'd be able to find all the monsters in the game right then and there. You're going to have to explore a lot if you want to see all the monsters there are to catch in the game. A good tip to remember, though, is that Pokémon tend to appear in places where there are a lot of people around, so places like shopping malls, big chain stores, convenience stops, and more. That's why it's a good idea to go with a trusted family member or adult if they ask you to help them run errands, so you can check out all the new Pokémon lurking there.

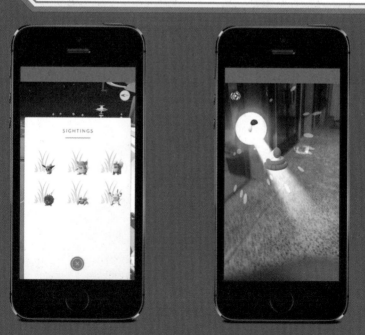

So many Pokémon to catch!

Remember, just because a Pokémon isn't in the Sightings menu, doesn't mean that it won't appear for catching, like Ekans did here.

To help you catch Pokémon, you're going to need more than just luck and some good athletic shoes. You'll need specialized items like lures that can help make Pokémon appear.

Here's what lures look like in the menu.

An up-close look at a Pokéstop that's been powered with a lure.

Lots of Pokémon are attracted to my incense and lures at these PokéStops.

But without them, you might not find or catch many Pokémon.

LURES

Now that you know how to navigate the map, it's time to start using lures. Lures are items that can be found from accomplishing certain things in the game like visiting PokéStops or leveling up, or by purchasing them in the shop with PokéCoins. To use a lure, you need to visit a Pokéstop and attach that lure to it. The lure will be active for thirty minutes, and everyone who is playing the game near that Pokéstop will be able to benefit from its effects. Only one lure can be used at a time at a Pokéstop.

All of these nearby PokéStops have been powered up with lures.

You can tell because pink petals are falling down from the Pokestop.

Now it's a Pokémon party. Who could ask for more?

When a lure is in place, you'll start to notice more Pokémon appear near it than normal. You can tell if a Pokémon appeared because of a lure if there are purple rings underneath it. One important thing to keep in mind is that the effects of lures can only be felt at that Pokéstop right then and there, so if you leave the area, you won't be able to reap that lure's benefits anymore.

After I left those PokéStops, I noticed very few Pokémon around.

I did see a Pidgey, but he only appeared because of normal circumstances. You can tell because there are white rings under the bird.

Keep that in mind that if you're going to be moving around a lot, and you want to use lures at different PokéStops, that's going to take up a lot of time. You want to use your lures wisely.

Seeing all these Pokémon are great,
but I'm not going to be in this area for long,
so it wouldn't be a good idea to set
a lure at these PokéStops again.

What's for certain is that lures make more Pokémon appear than normal. What's more difficult to say is if lures will make rarer Pokémon appear. There have been times when I've used lures, or have been near PokéStops that had lures, and have only seen common Pokémon appear.

This Growlithe is pretty high CP, but is still a common Pokémon in my neck of the woods.

There have been other times, though, when I've used a lure and been surprised to see rare Pokémon turn up. What happens at one powered up lure vs. another won't ever be a hundred percent alike, but you will see more Pokémon than you would have normally.

What is certain is that you'll still encounter a lot of Pidgeys whether you're using a lure or not.

Keep in mind that what you think of as a rare Pokémon isn't always going to be a rare Pokémon to someone else. Most Pokémon GO players would be excited to catch a Venosaur in the wild. But while you might not be stoked by an Eevee appearing in your area, another person who isn't from there might be excited to see an Eevee. If you go hang out near the ocean, you might be happy to encounter a Poliwhirl, but other people who live there might see them on a daily basis.

I see Eevees all the time in the wild, even though other players don't see them often.

INCENSE

The other item that help make Pokémon appear is incense, which can be gained by completing challenges in the game or by purchasing them in the shop. They last for thirty minutes, like lures, and make more Pokémon appear than normally would have. Like lures, there's a way you can tell if a Pokémon appeared because of an incense.

I'm using an incense here, but that isn't why this Zubat showed up.

And it's hard to tell if my incense had a big effect on this Rhyhorn showing up.

Just look to see if there's a purple cloud under that Pokémon. That means they showed up because of the incense.

Even though there are lures activated here, you can tell the Vulpix showed up because of my incense, since there is a purple cloud underneath him.

Same thing with this Mankey. You can see the thick, purple cloud of smoke surrounding it.

That's where the similarities between incense and lures stop. Unlike lures, incense can be used wherever you go, so if you ran across a football field with an incense, you'd still be able to see its effects no matter where you are.

This area is full of PokéStops, but if I used a lure on them, I could only feel the effects of those I was nearby. So it might be better to use a lure right now if I'm going to be walking a lot.

Incense can only effect you, not other players like lures can. So if you're walking down the street next to another person playing Pokémon GO and that person had an active incense, you wouldn't be able to experience any of its effects. Incenses are also slightly cheaper in the shop at eighty PokéCoins, while lures cost a hundred.

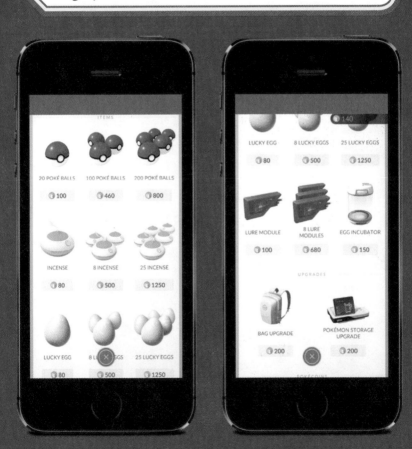

Lures are only twenty more PokéCoins than incense, but since PokéCoins are hard to come by, you need to think twice about which one to purchase.

It's hard to say whether lures or incense are more effective than the other at making more, or rare, Pokémon appear. You might use an incense one time and see fifteen Pokémon appear, and use it another time and see much less.

It's uncommon for a Pidgeot to appear on its own, unlike Pidgeys or Pidgeottos. But my incense had nothing to do with it.

You could use a lure and encounter rare Pokémon you never expected to find one time, and then see nothing out of the ordinary the next time.

Still no Pokémon around, even with my incense working.

From my experience, using both at the same time certainly can make more Pokémon appear than if you had only used one or neither. At the same time, there won't be a huge amount more Pokémon than if you had only used just an incense or a lure.

This Zubat appeared when I was using both, but it's hard to tell if it showed up because of the incense or the lure, or neither.

What you should remember, though, is that incense is best when you're going to be moving around a lot, and lures when you're going to be in the same spot at a Pokéstop. If you're going to be walking through a park, use an incense. If you're going to be sitting down on a bench and eating lunch at a park, use a lure.

There's nothing really around my area here, but I know I'm going to be walking a lot. I'll want to use an incense.

There are a lot of PokéStops within sitting distance, and I know I'm going to be here longer than thirty minutes. I'll want to use a lure.

One of the single most important things that PokéStops have to do with catching is giving you items. Any PokéStop you visit that's colored light blue will give items if you spin it. And you can spin it again to get more items; you just have to wait five minutes.

What a PokéStop looks like when you first approach it.

Some PokéStops have additional information.

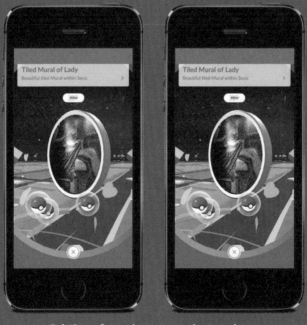

A PokéStop after you've spun it and retrieved items.

You could sit near a PokéStop all day and spin it to collect lots of items, or you could explore your city or town to find more. Regardless of how many you visit, each PokéStop will provide items, including Poké Balls, which are needed to catch Pokémon.

Three Poké Balls may not seem like much, but they add up quickly.

PokéStops with lures attached to them will bring in more Pokémon than those that don't. But PokéStops in general don't necessarily make Pokémon appear more than if you weren't near one.

Remember what we went over earlier, how busy places are where you're going to find a lot of different types of Pokémon? At those busy places is where you'll likely encounter lots of PokéStops, and where you will probably see a lot of people playing the game and a lot of Pokémon appearing nearby.

I visited this busy shopping mall on Sunday when a lot of people were around. Needless to say, there were lots of Pokémon, ready to catch.

Look for and think about areas where there are going to be a lot of people playing Pokémon, and that's where you'll find a lot of PokéStops to get items and see more monsters than you would normally be able to. If there's an outdoor market in a central part of your city that a lot of people GO to, you will probably see lots of people on their phone playing Pokémon GO, lots of PokéStops that have been powered up with lures, and in general, lots of Pokémon appearing.

In just thirty minutes, these were just some of the Pokémon that appeared at the mall.

And just twenty feet outside the mall I saw even more. It was easily the most I ever saw at one time, and that's not counting the ones that may have appeared when I wasn't looking at my phone.

None of these Pokémon are exactly "rare," but it shows you how important visiting new areas can be when it comes to catching new types of monsters. Places with lots of people are where you're going to find more Pokémon, and more PokéStops to get items.

CHAPTER 4

HATCHING EGGS AND EVOLVING MONSTERS TO GET RARE POKÉMON

Catching is just one of the main ways to collect Pokémon. The other two are hatching eggs and evolving monsters you already have. Eggs are items you collect from playing the game, and inside is a Pokémon that you can hatch. The way you do this is by selecting an egg with an egg incubator, and then walking, jogging or running a certain distance to make them open.

Here you can see all the eggs in my collection, the walking distances required to make them hatch, and which are being incubated.

Here's what an egg looks like when we select in on the menu.

After you select an incubator on an egg, it will look like this.

Eggs are designated by one of three distances: 2 km, 5 km or 10 km. 10 km eggs have the ability to hatch rarer Pokémon than 2 or 5 km eggs. Keep in mind that what one person considers a rare Pokémon isn't necessarily a rare Pokémon for someone else. I wasn't too excited when I hatched an Eevee after walking all over the place with a 10 km egg, especially since I see Eevees pretty frequently. But I was very happy when I got a Psyduck with a 5 km egg, since I hadn't ever encountered a Psyduck once before while playing the game.

That Psyduck is still the only one I have in my collection.

Eggs, though, don't necessarily hatch Pokémon that you wouldn't have been able to catch in the wild. I caught an Onix in the game, even though that Pokémon can still be obtained by hatching eggs. While you can only start off with a Bulbasuar, Charmander, Squirtle or Pikachu at the beginning of the game, you can still catch them in the wild or hatch them from eggs as well. Think of eggs as either something you can do in the background of other things you're doing while playing the game, or an activity you can do on its own to get more Pokémon.

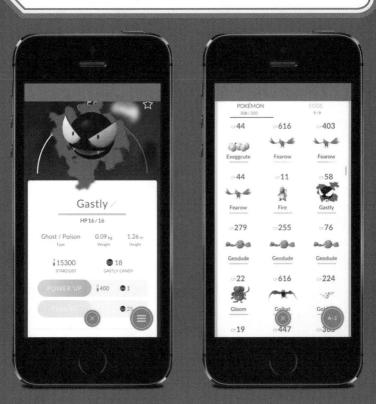

I got my only Gastly by hatching it from an egg while I was walking around catching other Pokémon. I still haven't caught another Gastly.

But if you're wondering what type of Pokémon might appear from an egg you have, below is a good chart to give you an idea. This chart is based off of personal experience from hatching eggs, as well as information from Serebii.net, an online location that has lots of information about Pokémon GO and other Pokémon-related items.

Name of Pokémon	Distance		
Bulbasaur	2 km	Ekans	5 km
Charmander	2 km	Sandshrew	5 km
Squirtle	2 km	Nidoran (male)	5 km
Caterpie	2 km	Nidoran (female)	5 km
Weedle	2 km	Vulpix	5 km
Pidgey	2 km	Oddish	5 km
Rattata	2 km	Paras	5 km
Spearow	2 km	Venonat	5 km
Pikachu	2 km	Diglett	5 km
Clefairy	2 km	Meowth	5 km
Jigglypuff	2 km	Psyduck	5 km
Zubat	2 km	Mankey	5 km
Geodude	2 km	Growlithe	5 km
Magikarp	2 km	Poliwag	5 km

Abra	5 km	Tangela	5 km
Machop	5 km	Horsea	5 km
Bellsprout	5 km	Goldeen	5 km
Tentacool	5 km	Staryu	5 km
Poynta	5 km	Porygon	5 km
Slowpoke	5 km	Onix	10 km
Magnemite	5 km	Hitmonlee	10 km
Doduo	5 km	Hitmonchan	10 km
Seel	5 km	Scyther	10 km
Grimer	5 km	Jynx	10 km
Shellder	5 km	Electabuzz	10 km
Gastly	5 km	Magmar	10 km
Drowzee	5 km	Pinsir	10 km
Krabby	5 km	Lapras	10 km
Voltorb	5 km	Eevee	10 km
Exeggcute	5 km	Omanyte	10 km
Cubone	5 km	Kabuto	10 km
Lickitung	5 km	Aerodactyl	10 km
Koffing	5 km	Snorlax	10 km
Rhyhorn	5 km	Dratini	10 km

Something to note is that 5 km eggs seem to hatch the most diverse group of Pokémon. 10 km eggs hatch a lot of Pokémon that are great in battle and aren't easily found in the wild, but still some of them can be found pretty easily: Eevees are relatively common to catch, and Dratinis can be found at major landmarks and historical sites, so go to one of those and you can probably find one. But if you're looking to use all of those Dratinis' Candy to eventually evolve one into a Dragonair and then a Dragonite, waiting to hatch a 10 km egg to hopefully get a Dratini and then hoping to evolve them will take a lot longer than just finding them in the wild.

What we can also see from this chart is that there are some Pokémon who make more sense to try and get them from egg hatching than catching them in the wild. Lapras is a rare water Pokémon that doesn't appear as often as, say, Squirtle does. So if you don't actually live near a body of water or can't get to one easily, finding Lapras in the wild is going to be very hard. But if you have a few 10 km eggs and some time to actually walk and hatch them, you could get a Lapras much more quickly.

Kabutops is also an interesting case. You can't actually hatch a Kabutops, and depending on your location, finding one in the wild can be very difficult. But it is easier, though, to catch and hatch Kabuto with a 10 km egg, and then use that Candy to evolve it into a Kabutops.

Aerodactyls are also pretty rare and don't actually evolve from anything, so you can't necessarily capture lots of a lesser Pokémon in hopes of evolving one of them into an Aerodactyl. That's why hatching a 10 km egg is probably the best way of going about getting this Pokémon, especially if you have trouble finding it in the wild.

So with so many rare Pokémon available in 5-10 km eggs, what's the purpose of even hatching a 2 km egg to begin with? You could still find Pidgey or Rattata pretty regularly in the game, so why even waste that footwork on a 2 km egg when you could be using it for a 5-10 km one?

Oh boy, I can't wait to see what Pokémon I hatch.

Another Meowth? Oh well.

There are two reasons why you should still focus on hatching smaller eggs: 1. Hatching eggs generates XP, and if you're looking to get to that next level quickly, hatching a 2 km egg could help out a lot. And 2. Because 2 km eggs can hatch Bulbasaurs, Charmanders, and Squirtles, and you'll need their Candy if you want them to reach their final form of Venosaur, Charizard or Blastoise, respectively. Bulbasaurs, Charmanders, and Squirtles, while still being found more frequently in certain areas, aren't as common as Weedles, Pidgeys, Zubats, or other lower-level Pokémon. And you can still find their final evolved forms in the wild. But hatching those 2 km eggs to get more of them will help you get more of those Pokémon in your ranks to evolve them into something better. Every 2 km egg will hatch a Pokémon that can evolve into a different monster.

They may not look like much, but these Pokémon can evolve into much stronger monsters.

This same concept applies to 5 km eggs—even if you hatch something that's at the beginning of an evolution process, you can still evolve it into something better later on. But the difference between the type of Pokémon you get from 5 km eggs vs. 2 km eggs is that the Pokémon you're given are more rare in general than those in 2 km. Gastly can be hatched from a 5 km egg, and with enough of its Candy can evolve into Haunter and then Gangar. But finding a Gastly in the wild will likely be more difficult than coming across a Spearow or a Pikachu. What's rare to one person isn't necessarily rare to someone else, but being able to hatch Staryus, Koffings, Voltorbs, Magnemites, Porygons and more from 5 km eggs makes that much less work you have to do in the wild to find them.

I don't have to worry about catching another Koffing now since I hatched mine from an egg.

So which eggs should you hatch at any given moment? That depends on your situation. If there's a specific Pokémon you're trying to hatch, try to hatch as many of its eggs as possible. If you're looking to get Pokémon that are more uncommon and can evolve into even more rare Pokémon, 5 km eggs are the way to go. If you want to catch some of the most rare Pokémon available and don't mind working your legs out in the process, then you'll want to hatch 10 km eggs. You can do one of each at a time or three of the same egg type all together—just remember what your goals are when hatching them.

I have some free time and a lot to explore,
so now would be a good time to focus on hatching a 5 or 10 km egg.

One thing to remember, though, is that there are certain Pokémon that are believed to be only available in geographic regions in the world when the game first started: Tauros is only available in North America, Mr. Mime in Europe, Farfetch'd in parts of Asia, and Kangashkan in Australia. Plus, there are legendary Pokémon like Zapdos or Mewtwo that haven't been made available to the mass public yet as of August. That means if there's somebody you know at school who says they've captured all of the Pokémon, they're probably lying, since they'd have had to travel the world or traded with another player whose travelled that far to encounter all of those creatures.

Just get into a steady habit of hatching eggs: as soon as you get a new one, begin trying to hatch it, and when you're finished, start another again. You don't want to be out playing the game without an egg incubating. That would be wasting footwork. And if you're conflicted on whether you want to jog around the park or ride your bike up and down the street to hatch an egg, just remember that the best way to hatch them is by walking in a straight line down a long sidewalk or path.

See how the streets in this map wind and curve a lot? It probably isn't the best place to try and hatch eggs, since the game might not count my distance walked accurately.

But this street is straight and goes on for a while, so it'd be a good place for me to walk and try and hatch eggs.

The game determines how much distance you've travelled by regularly checking in on where you were at one point in time vs. another. So if you're running up and down the same street over and over again, the game might only read that as you running a shorter distance than you actually did. If you're biking around the park, you might end up going too fast and the game might not reward you for the distance travelled, since it might think you're in a car. But simply walking down a long street or some other long path in a straight line, although a bit more time-consuming and maybe less convenient, is the best way to ensure that you don't lose out on any footwork and that the app accurately rewards you that distance for eggs.

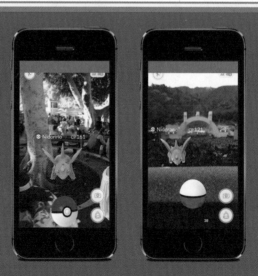

Plus, during all that walking, you'll be able to take some pretty cool pictures, like I did when I was hatching eggs while walking to a concert.

EVOLVING POKÉMON

The final piece of collecting the Pokémon puzzle is evolving, where certain Pokémon, with enough of their respective Candy, can be evolved into different and even stronger Pokémon. When you evolve a Pokémon, you get an entirely new one and lose the one that you started off with.

Evolving Geodude gave me Graveler, an entirely new Pokémon.

To begin the evolution process, you'll need enough of that Pokémon's Candy, which can be gained by capturing them in the wild, or transferring them back to Professor Willow. Each Pokémon has its own specific Candy, so Pikachu Candy can't help a Charmander evolve. But each Pokémon in a specific evolutionary chain uses the same Candy, so Squirtle, Wartortle and Blastoise all use the same Squirtle Candy to power up.

Evolving plays a bigger role in battling, as Pokémon that are evolved are usually more powerful than those that aren't. For collecting Pokémon, though, evolving's main purpose is to get Pokémon you don't already have. You can still capture an evolved Pokémon in the wild that you've evolved from your collection.

Only one of these Pidgeots came from catching. The others came from evolving.

The question is, which Pokémon should we spend time to evolve? The answer to that question would be different if we were focusing on battling in this book, but for purposes of just catching Pokémon, we'll want to evolve as many as possible, while still leaving at least one unevolved version of each so we can say we have them in our collection. Plus, evolving any Pokémon gets XP, which helps you level up quicker and become a better player in the game.

CHAPTER 5
THE MOST DIFFICULT POKÉMON TO CATCH

Pokémon can appear anywhere, regardless of where you are on the map. But certain types of Pokémon have a tendency to appear in certain areas, and some Pokémon might be more rare or difficult to catch, regardless of what CP they are at or if they have a red ring around them. Pidgeys, Caterpies, and Zubats, while being more difficult to catch in some situations than others, are generally easier to catch than, say, Charizards, Venosaurs, or Blastoises. A good general rule is the more rare the Pokémon, the harder it will be to catch it.

This Charmeleon was more difficult to catch, since it's rarer than its lesser-evolved Charmander.

But which ones in particular are harder to catch than others? The Silph Road has the answer. The Silph Road is a comprehensive online community of Pokémon GO players who've come together to try and figure out some of the most difficult puzzles of the game and how the game works in general. With a trusted adult, you can visit TheSilphRoad.com, TheSilphRoad.com/research, or reddit.com/r/thesilphroad to find out more information about a specific Pokémon GO question you may have.

But here are the most difficult Pokémon to capture, organized from most difficult to least.

DIFFICULTY	POKÉMON NAME
Most difficult	Venusaur, Blastoise, Charizard, Dragonite
2nd most	Ivysaur, Charmeleon, Wartortle, Raichu, Clefable, Ninetales, Arcanine, Gyrados, Dragonair, Gengar
3rd most	Butterfree, Beedrill, Pidgeot, Nidoking, Nidoqueen, Poliwrath, Alakazam, Machamp, Victreebell, Golem
4th most	Vileplume, Rapidash, Marowak, Vaporeon, Jolteon, Flareon, Omastar, Kabutops
5th most	Raticate, Fearow, Arbok, Sandslash, Wigglytuff, Golbat, Parasect, Venomoth, Dugtrio, Persian, Golduck, Primeape, Tentacruel, Slowbro, Magneton, Dodrio, Dewgong, Muk, Cloyster, Haunter, Hypno, Kingler, Electrode, Exeggutor, Weezing, Rhydon, Seadra, Seaking, Starmie, Bulbasaur, Charmander, Squirtle, Pikachu, Hitmonlee, Hitmonchan, Lickitung, Chansey, Lapras, Ditto, Aerodactyl, Snorlax, Kangaskhan, Onix

6th most	Metapod, Kakuna, Pidgeotto, Nidorina, Nidorino, Poliwhirl, Kadabra, Machoke, Weepinbell, Graveler
7th most	Gloom, Clefairy, Vulpix, Growlithe, Farfetch'd, Mr. Mime, Scyther, Jynx, Electabuzz, Magmar, Pinsir, Tauros
8th most	Paras, Ponyta, Gastly, Cubone, Tangela, Eevee, Porygon, Omanyte, Kabuto, Dratini
9th most	Caterpie, Weedle, Pidgey, Rattata, Spearow, Ekans, Sandshrew, Nidoran, (both types), Jigglypuff, Zubat, Venonat, Diglett, Meowth, Psyduck, Mankey, Poliwag, Abra, Machop, Bellsprout, Tentacool, Geodude, Slowpoke, Magnemite, Doduo, Seel, Grimer, Shellder, Drowzee, Krabby, Voltorb, Exeggcute, Koffing, Rhyhorn, Horsea, Goldeen, Staryu
10th most	Oddish
11th most	Magikarp

Some of the stuff on this chart seems fairly obvious. Venusaurs, Blastoises, Charizards, and Dragonites are some of the hardest Pokémon to evolve since you need so much of their Candy, so it'd make sense that they're the most difficult regular Pokémon to catch. And Magikarp is essentially a dud Pokémon—it doesn't really have much use until it evolves into the more menacing Gyrados, so it makes sense that it'd be easiest to catch. And the more common Pokémon you see in the wild, like Caterpie, Pidgey, Ekans, Zubat, and both Nidorans, are some of the easier ones to capture.

The fact that I have so many Pidgeys, Rattatas, and Ekans can attest to this.

But let's look at the "5th most" row on the chart. You'll notice Pokémon like Ratticate, Fearow, Arbok, and Golbat there, the evolved versions of the common Pokémon Rattata, Spearow, Ekans, and Zubat. These Pokémon are fairly easy to evolve and are relatively common for many players, so you'd probably have a better shot getting a Fearow or Golbat by evolving from a Spearow or Zubat than by trying to catch one in the wild. This doesn't mean you shouldn't try to catch one in the wild; it just means that you might not be successful in catching one, while evolving from a lower-level Pokémon will do the trick for sure.

I ended up getting my Sandslash, a Pokémon in the "5th most" row, from evolving, since I couldn't find it in the wild.

You can also see in the "7th most" row of the chart that Pokémon like Magmar, Electabuzz, and Scyther are there. What's interesting about this is that these Pokémon are among those that can be hatched from 10 km eggs, literally the most time- and walk-intensive ones to hatch. Scyther, Magmar, and Electabuzz are generally more rare to catch than Caterpies or Cubones, but it's interesting to see that they aren't necessarily that difficult to catch in the wild compared to other Pokémon, even though they take a while to hatch. This means that if you ever run across one of these in the wild, do everything you can to catch it, and then you might be able to avoid having to walk 10 km to hatch one open in an egg.

I hatched my Electabuzz from an egg, but I wish I had found it in the wild instead.

Again, every situation is different when catching. You might notice you have no problem catching a Charmeleon even though it's one of the more difficult ones to catch, or you could throw five Poké Balls and still never catch a Caterpie, despite it being one of the easiest. But this should serve as a good guide for which Pokémon will give you bigger trouble in the game.

WHERE TO FIND RARE POKÉMON

You probably won't find all of the Pokémon just by sitting at your house or sticking to your neighborhood; you're actually going to have to get out and explore to find more. Pokémon types can help play into where they will appear. Here's a good rundown of where you can expect to find certain types of Pokémon:

Water: Oceans, reservoirs, ponds, beaches, rivers, canals. If there's water near you, you will probably find water Pokémon there.

Grass: Large areas of grass, forests, parks, fields, golf courses—essentially, areas where there's a lot of open field and areas of grass about.

Bug: Pretty similar to grass Pokémon: large fields, parks, golf courses, fields—anywhere with lots of greenery and grass.

Fire: Residential areas like neighborhoods and suburbs, cities, and places that might be more hot or dry, like close to the desert or Southern California.

Rock: Outdoorsy areas like trails, open fields. Others can include shopping malls, parking structures.

Ground: Urban areas, outdoorsy areas, open fields.

Electric: Industrial/urban areas, cities, college campuses, schools.

Fighting: Stadiums, arenas.

Poison: Wetlands, industrial areas.

Fairy: Churches, cemeteries, notable landmarks, historic locations.

Flying: Grassy areas, fields, gardens, parks, forests.

Dragons: Notable landmarks, historic locations.

Ghost: Churches, parking lots at night, residential areas at night.

Ice: Grassy areas, bodies of water, colder areas.

Psychic: Grassy areas, residential areas at night, hospitals.

Steel: Train tracks, train stations, industrial areas.

Some of these areas are more common to get to than others, like parks, open fields, or urban areas, and that's why you see a lot of specific types appear more often there. Other places, like large bodies of water, aren't always next door, so you'll actually have to plan out some traveling to get to them. While these are good guidelines for what Pokémon are more likely to appear in one area vs. another, they aren't necessarily a hundred percent, surefire way to find that Pokémon you've been looking for.

I was happy to get this Rhydon, even though I was looking for an Ivysaur.

There've been times when I've seen a Charmeleon appear, even though I was nowhere near an industrial or arid area. And other times, Rock Pokémon have appeared, despite me being nowhere near a shopping mall or a big parking structure. Sometimes I've gone by churches and have never seen a Clefairy, and then the next time I go to a church, I'll see two or three. You're going to have to keep exploring everywhere you can to find Pokémon. It's also why you should keep hatching eggs as much as possible: I know that I don't have easy access to train tracks or industrial areas to find a Magnemite, but I do know that I have lots of 5 km eggs and free time to walk and hatch them in hopes of getting one.

I didn't expect to see this Jolteon or Machoke when I was exploring the map, but was happy to add them to my collection.

CHAPTER 6
FINAL COMMENTS

In Pokémon GO and any other Pokémon game, catching and collecting all of the monsters is arguably the most impressive and most difficult challenge you can accomplish. There's no reason why you can't do so in Pokémon GO—you'll just have to put in a lot of time into playing the game, a lot of walking to hatch eggs, and a lot of exploration to find new areas to catch Pokémon.

Don't forget the fundamental three things you'll need to do to collect all the monsters: catch Pokémon, evolve Pokémon, and hatch Pokémon. There are some that are only available in certain regions of the world, as discussed earlier, and some that may not be available yet, so just focus on collecting all of the others for now. That way, when you do, you'll truly have caught them all and be a true master at Pokémon GO.